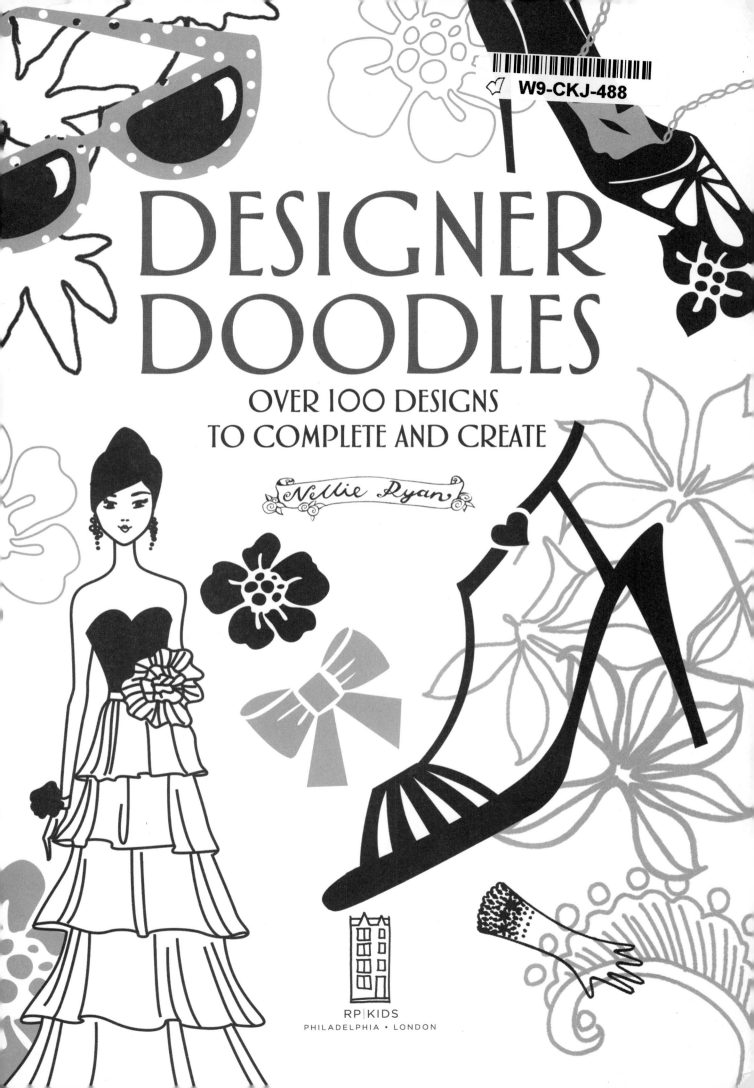

DESIGNER DOODLES

OVER 100 DESIGNS
TO COMPLETE AND CREATE

Nellie Ryan

RP | KIDS
PHILADELPHIA • LONDON

9   8
Digit on the right indicates the number of this printing

ISBN 978-0-7624-3761-0

Illustrated by Nellie Ryan

This edition published by Running Press Kids,
an imprint of
Running Press Book Publishers
2300 Chestnut Street
Philadelphia, PA 19103-4371

Visit us on the web!
www.runningpress.com

Viva la diva!

Design a diamond necklace that sparkles
like the star you are.

Add divine detail to this sleek gown
to take the red carpet by storm.

Floral frills and pretty prom queens.

Keep these pretty prom dresses
looking young and fresh, with fun frills.

Good old-fashioned glamor.

Design some show-stopping shoes.

Cover the dress with sparkles and complete the train
for an award-winning look.

The Charity Ball calls...

Design the invitation...

...and a must-have mask.

...for glamor for a good cause.

Finish these beautiful ball gowns.

Breathtaking bridesmaids...

Design two different looks for the bridesmaids.

...to a beautiful bride.

Finish the tiara.

Draw the bouquet from above.

Design her wonderful wedding dress and bouquet

The Christmas party.

Design a gorgeous handbag to go
with these festive dresses.

Give these dresses some Christmas sparkle.

April showers.

Draw a gorgeous pattern
for the raincoats...

...and one for the umbrellas.

Add a splash of color to spring,
with bright umbrellas and wild boots.

Down on the farm.

Design a cool cowboy hat...

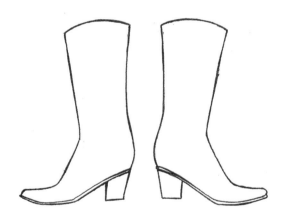

...and some great boots.

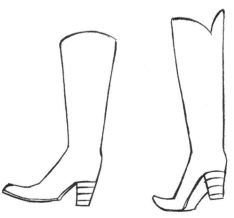

Give these cowgirls some jeans and
decorate their cowboy boots.

Tea for two.

*Design floral patterns
for the tea dresses.*

Give the dresses some divine detail.

Keep classic cardigans cute.

Cover the cardigans in beautiful embroidery and beads.

A day at the races.

You need a hat to stay ahead.

Design their hats to give their outfits some chapeau-chic.

Shorts and sweets.

Sassy shorts are the perfect way to stay cool.

Design some super-hot hot pants.

Decorate the
shopping bags.

Summer in the city.

Design the outfits for this girly getaway.

Ship ahoy!

Give these sassy seafaring gals
bold buttons and nautical stripes.

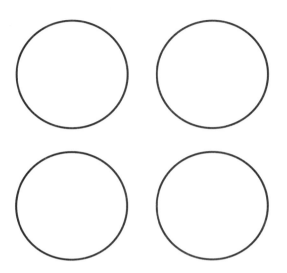

Design some buttons with a nautical theme. Detail is everything.

It's a jungle out there.

Gear up for summer with some super safari-wear. Give these girls cool combats, short-sleeved shirts, and sunhats.

The temperature is rising...

Skirts may be short, but accessories are big news.

...and so are the hemlines.

Team sassy skirts with bright bags, belts, sunhats and shades.

It's a shore thing.

Come up with a cute beach cover-up.

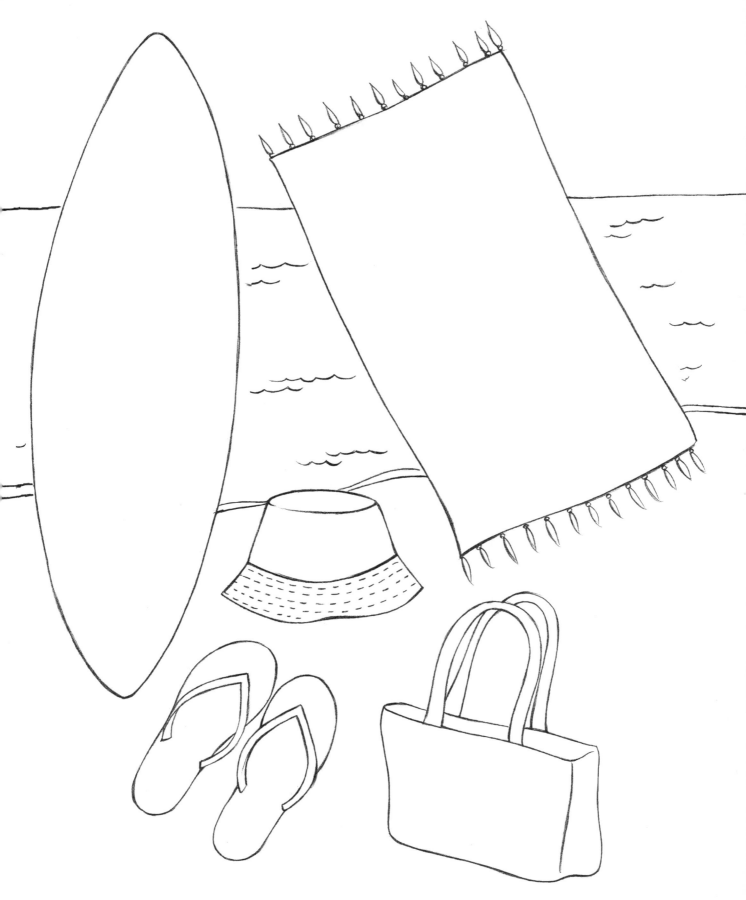

Set out into the sun in style with
your own range of beach accessories.

Damsels of the deep.

Dive right in and design this season's brilliant bathing suits and bikinis.

Short pants in—ankles out.

Design some cute calf-length pants.

Marvelous flip-flops.

Design some fun and fancy flip-flops.

Nights are drawing in.

Design a bright pattern for
the bag and one for the coat

Brighten up autumn days with a patterned coat
and contrasting bag.

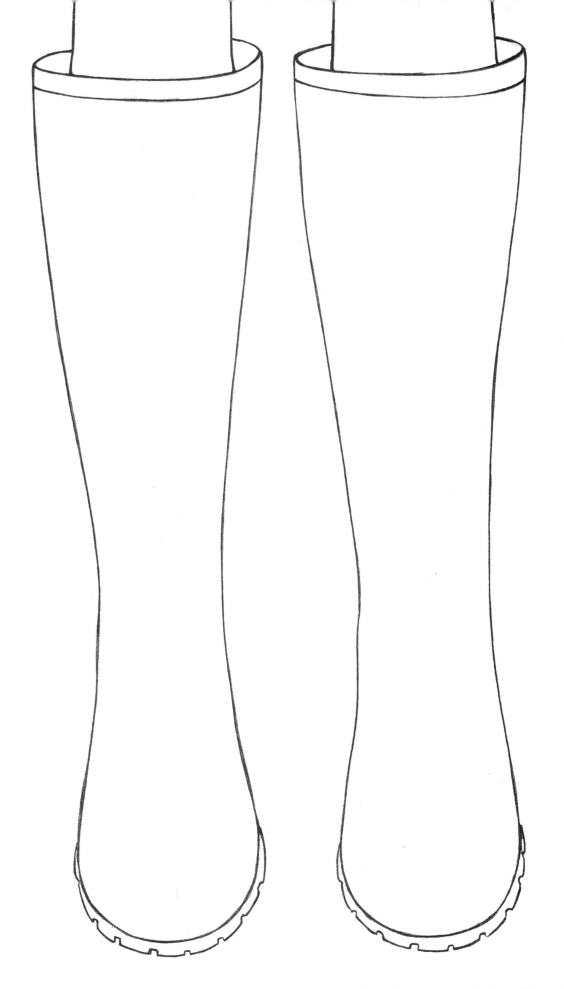

Add the perfect pair of printed boots to complete the look.

Up to your knees in style.

This season's boots are knee-high.

Design a collection of must-have boots.

Give these geek-chic girls pretty pleated skirts and tops.

Packing a poncho.

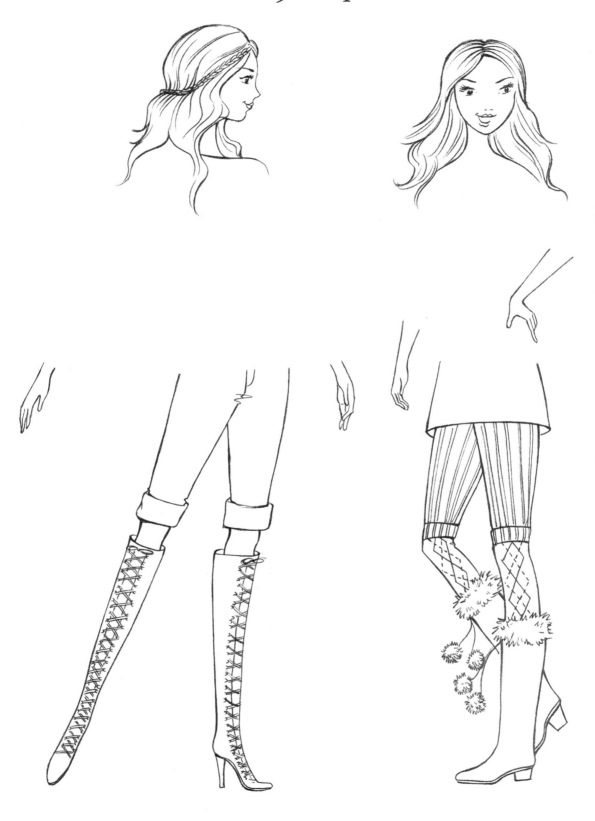

Sleeves are so last season.
Pep up these ponchos with punchy patterns.

Wools are essential this winter.

Give these girls some wooly sweaters, hats, and scarves.

Check them out.

Cover their outfits in tartans and checks.

City slickers.

Make these models look like they mean business
in sharp suits.

Top coats.

Finish these winter coats with some stylish buttons and lapels.

Fur is fine, as long as it's fake.

Finish these fabulous fake-fur jackets and coats.

Hit the slopes in style.

Design their ski jackets and winter boots.

Get fit to be seen.

Be fit and fabulous by designing your own range of gym-wear.

Green with envy.

Tee off in style with some gorgeous golf-wear.

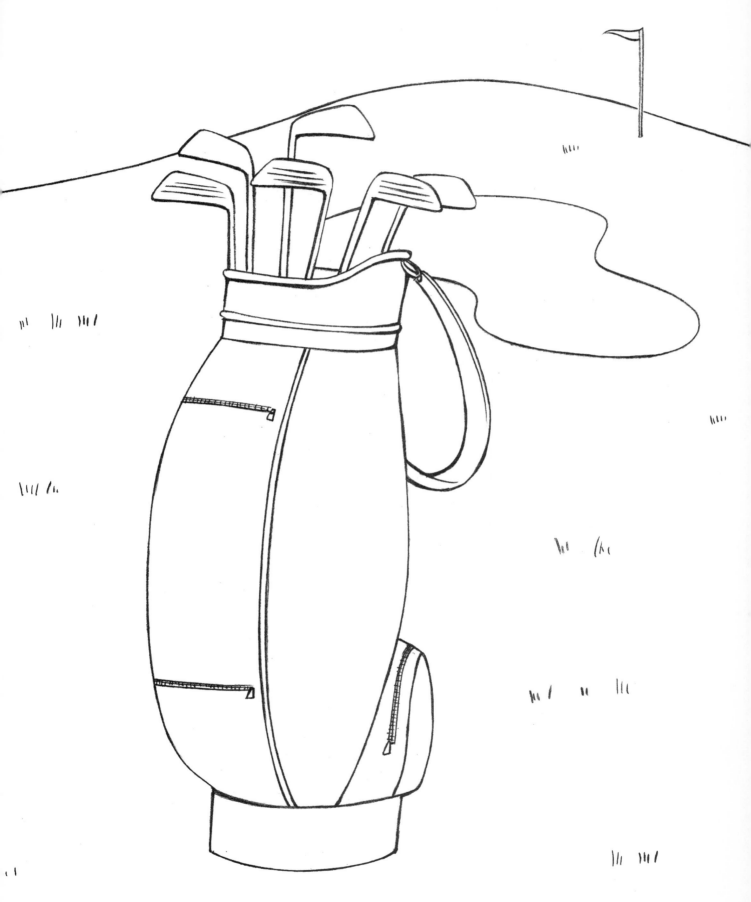

And a groovy golf bag.

Saddle up in style.

Design a collection of riding gear, and decorate the saddle.

Game, set and matching.

Give this designer doubles team desirable tennis whites.

Better skate than never.

Give these girls some super-stylish skater clothes
and decorate their boards.

Give us an "S," give us a "T," give us a "Y-L-E."

Give these cheerleaders some uniforms to shout about

Punk it up.

Give these punk princesses ripped T-shirts.

Sneakin' around.

Give these girls some sassy sneakers.

Bohemian rhapsody!

Team floaty skirts with gypsy jewels.

Ad-hoc frock.

Create the main pattern
for the fabric.

Add an "accent" pattern
for the sleeves.

Mix the bold patterns you've created for that thrown-together look.

Badges of honor.

Make a statement—cover the lapels with designer badges.

What statement do you want to make?

Design some badges and then cover the jacket

Born to ride.

The leather look is hot, on or off the road.

Give these biker babes some biker jackets and boots.
Don't forget to decorate the bike.

Rock-chick chic.

Rock and roll is never out of style. Make her outfit supercool with a band T-shirt and distressed jeans.

A bit of military magic.

Design your own camouflage and then cover her combat clothes.

Decorate this shirt, too.

Psychedelic patterns.

Cover the dress in this super psychedelic pattern

Neon brights and disco lights.

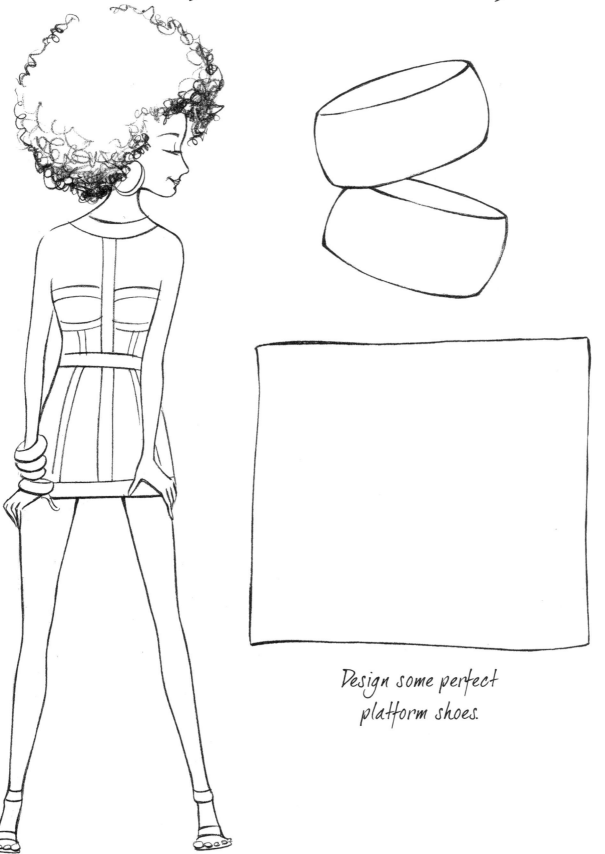

Design some perfect
platform shoes.

Grab your shades, you'll need them to see this season's designs.

Hitting the decks.

Decorate the DJ's dress for the disco.

Get the party in full swing.

Team terrific tassels with far-out fringing.

The ultimate party shoes.

Put the soul back into these party shoes.

Bring on the ballet pump.

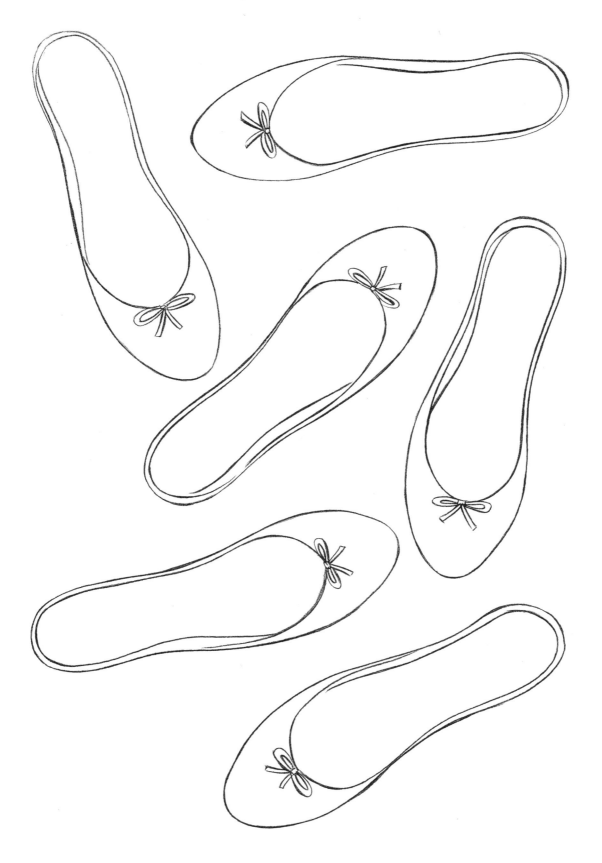

Put your best foot forward with this season's patterned pumps.

Design some terrific tights.

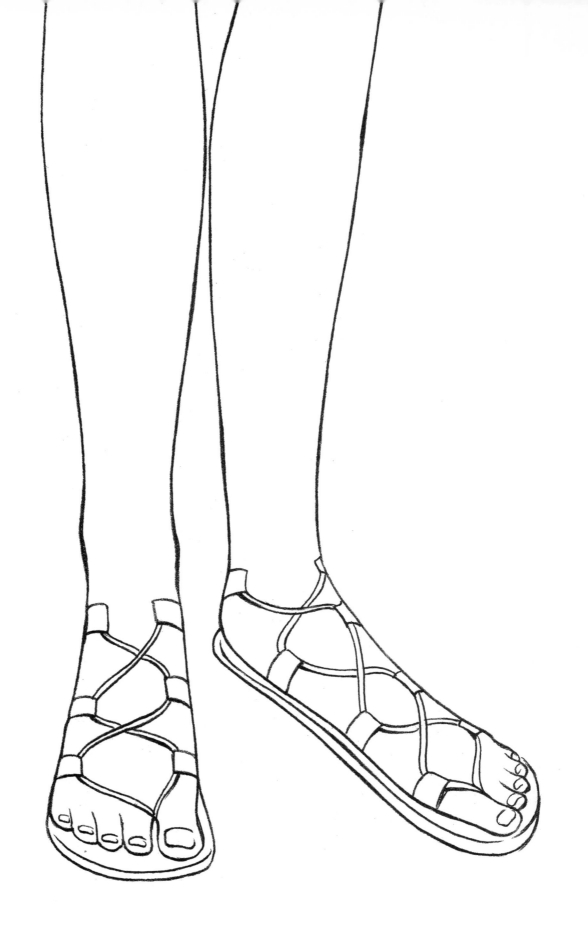

Lace up these sandals.

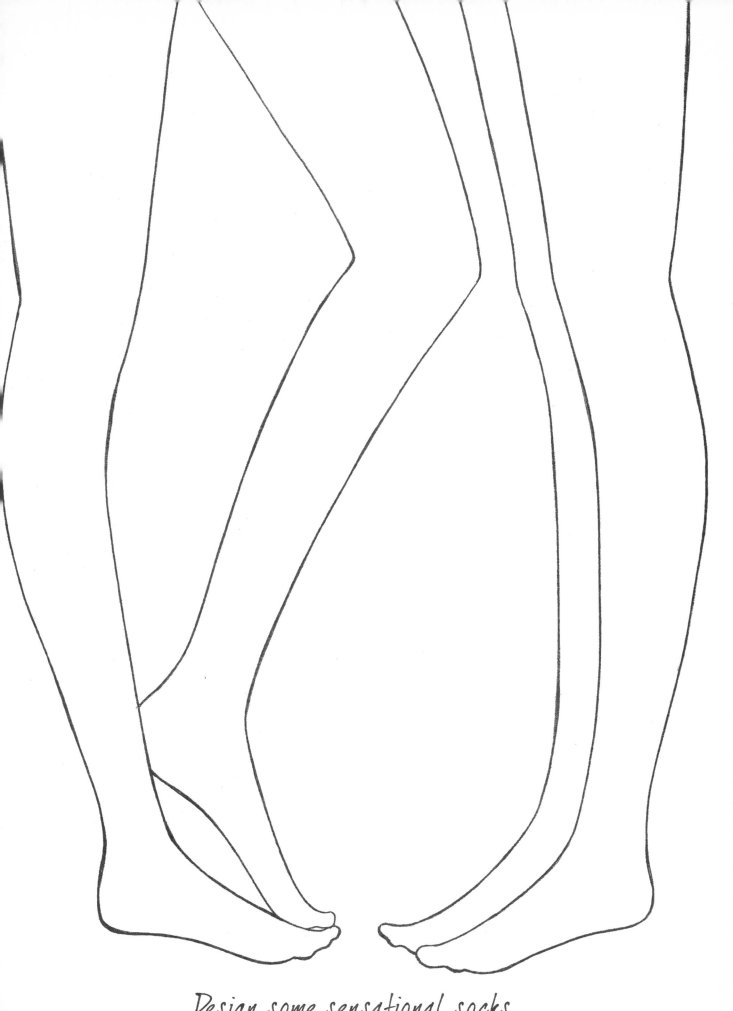

Design some sensational socks.

Get carried away...

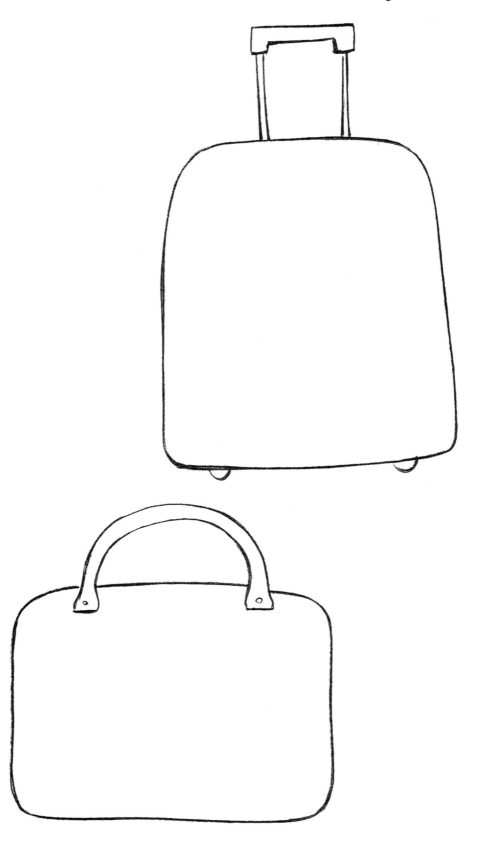

Make this baggage bright and beautiful.

...with this season's luggage collection.

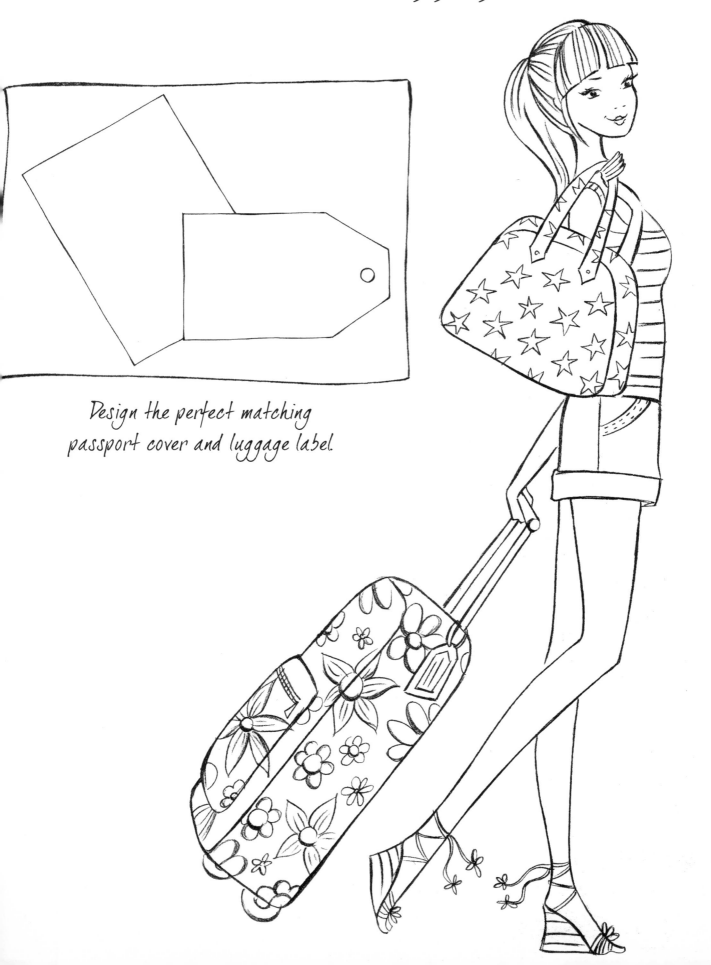

Design the perfect matching
passport cover and luggage label.

Must-have handbags.

Finish these fabulous handbags.

A bag to keep hold of.

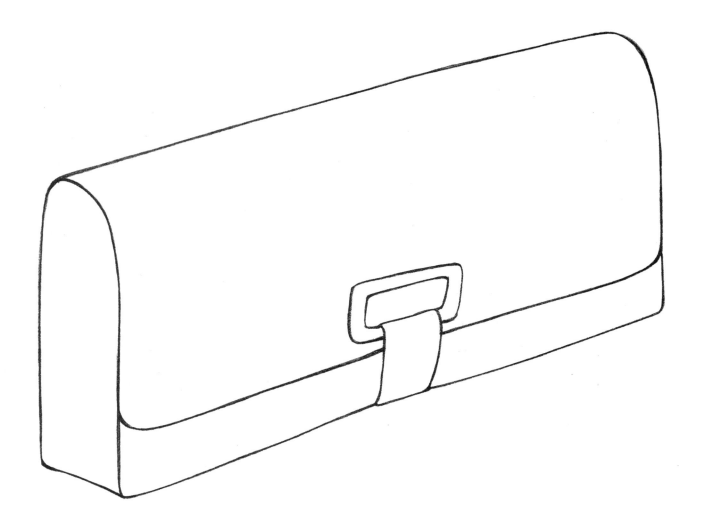

Make this clutch bag beautiful with beading.

And that's a wrap.

Design a collection of pretty scarves and pashminas.

Finish their outfits by adding detail to their wraps.

Bold bandanas.

Keep hair under control with these happening headscarves.
Finish the scarves and give them pretty patterns.

Desirable jewelery.

Design your own range of earrings.

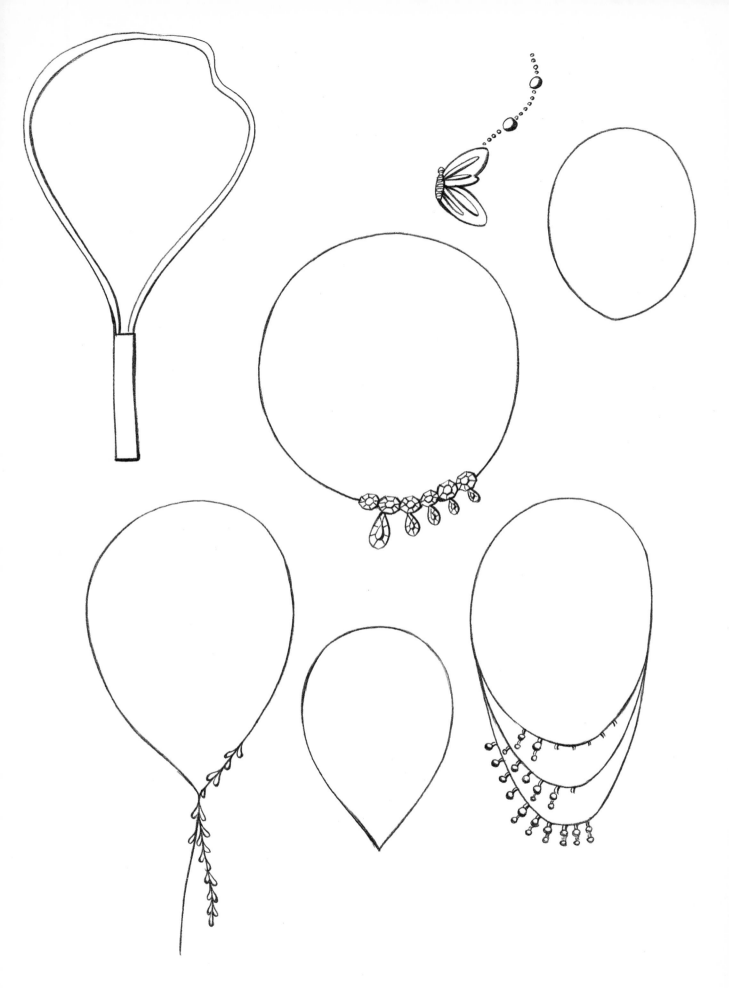

Finish these necklaces with beautiful pendants and beads.

Purrr-fect pet-wear.

Give these cool cats and precious pooches some style.

Cool shades.

Give her some shiny new sunglasses.

Get a grip.

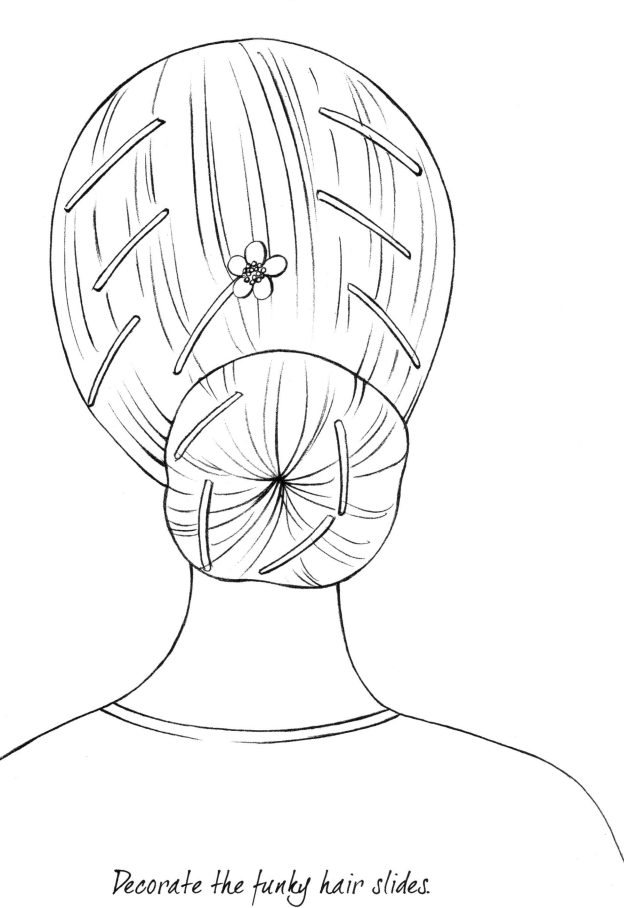

Decorate the funky hair slides.

Sleep tight.

Decorate her beautiful eye mask...

...and her gorgeous pajamas.

From fine...to fabulous.

Give the model a designer makeover.

It's show time.

Give the model dramatic catwalk make-up and hair.

Backstage at the fashion show.

Draw your own collection of catwalk clothes on the rail.

Finishing touches.

Get these models ready to take to the catwalk.

Make the finishing touches to their glamorous gowns.

Bangles and rings.

Draw the final outfit of the show.

Front-row seats.

What are they wearing on the front row of the fashion show?

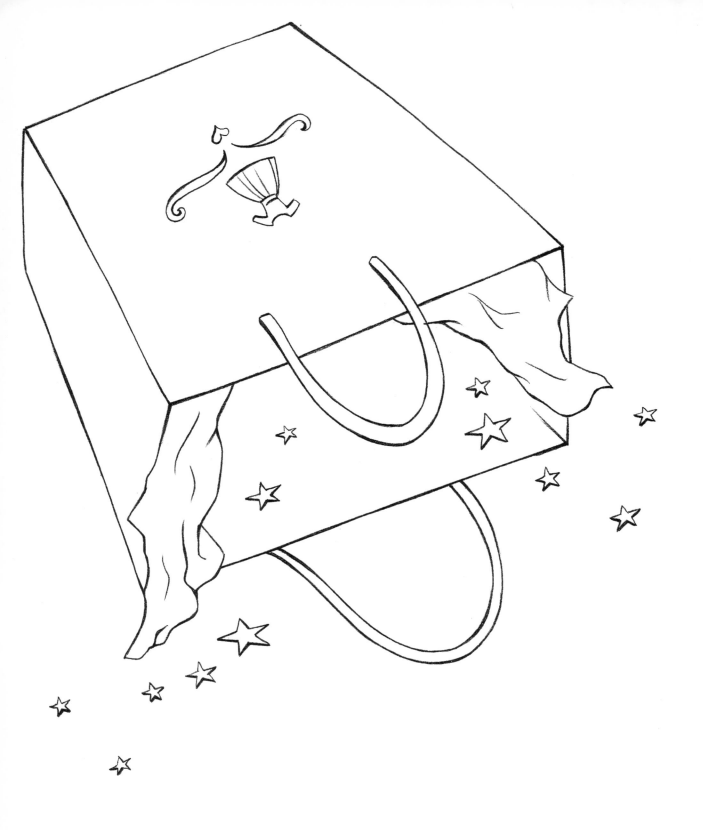

What's in the after-show party bag?

What's on the front cover of the fashion magazine?

Your designer fragrance.

Design the bottle.

Advertise your designer fragrance on the billboard.

Girls just want to have fun.

Style the girl band so they can be top of the fashion charts.

Kiss and make-up.

Design your own range of beauty products...

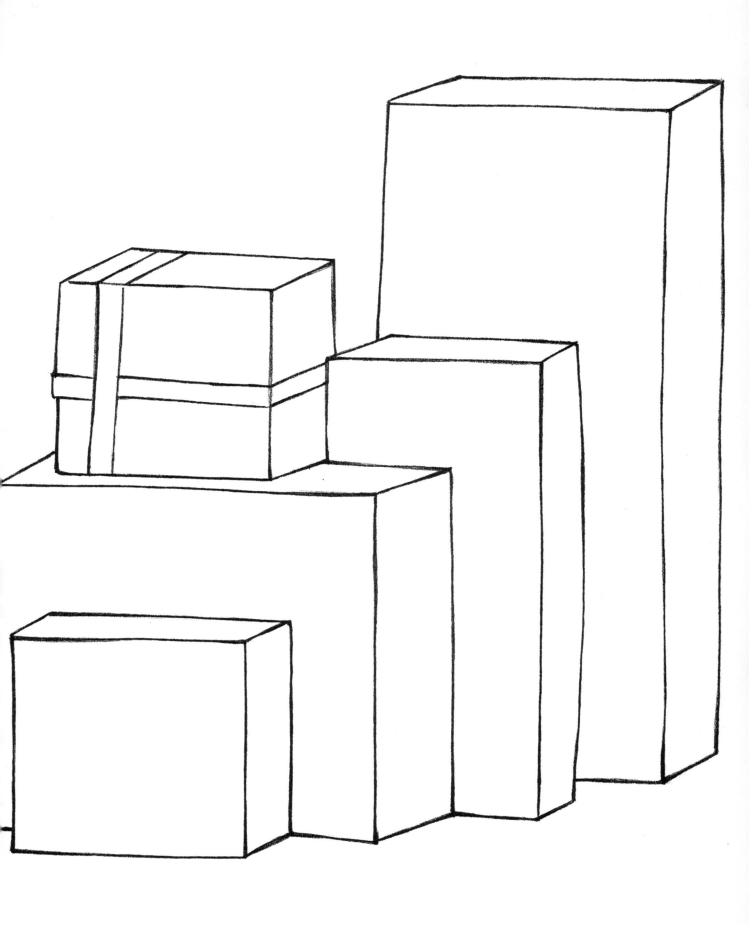

...with the prettiest packaging.

For the boys?

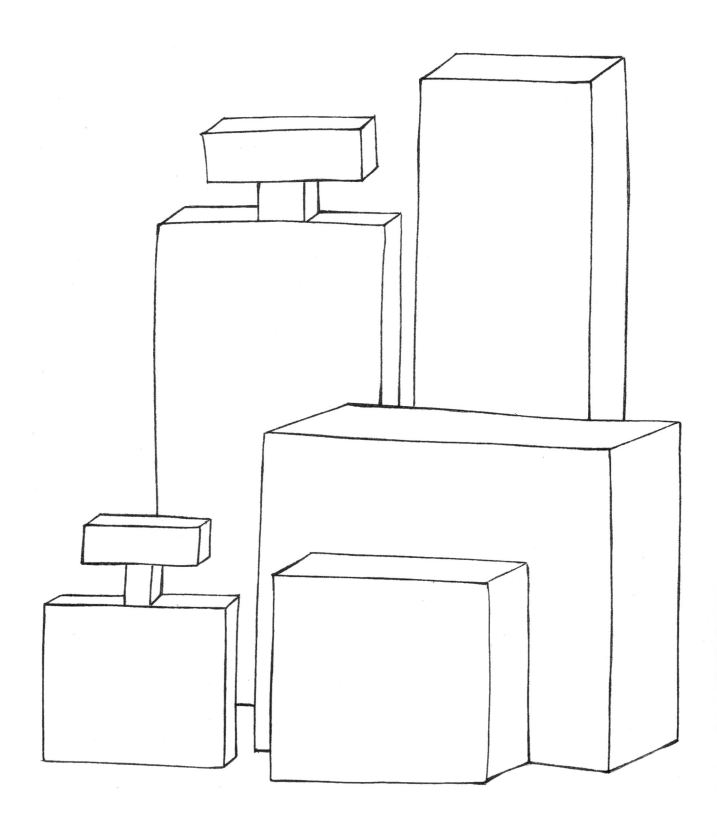

Design a product range for men.

Apply your beauty products...

...and some nail polish.

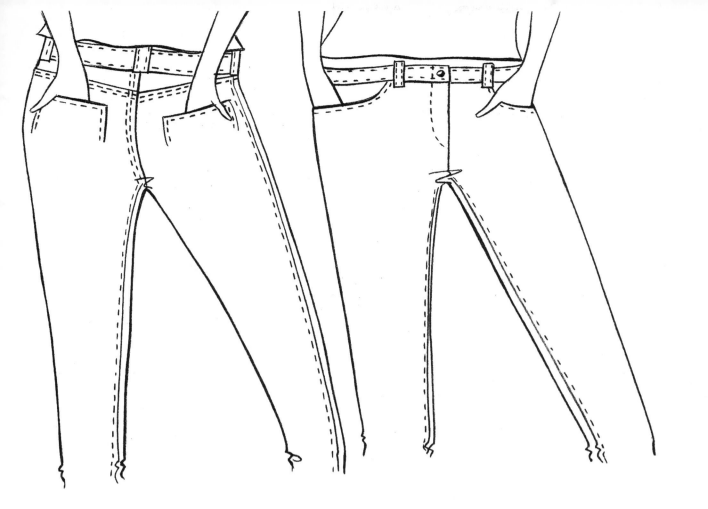

Skinny or flared for your designer denims?

On-trend T's.

Use bold letters to design your own range of signature T-shirts.

Draw the clothes in your shop window.

Your designer home.

Design your ideal home.

Your designer wardrobe.

Organize your designer clothes in the wardrobe.